AN EYE FOR AN EYE
A COLLECTION OF POEMS
BY ANNA LEEHEY

© All contents copyright by Anna Leehey. All rights reserved. All photos were taken by the author unless otherwise noted. No part of this document or the related files may be reproduced or transmitted in any form without the prior written permission of the author.

DEDICATION

This book is dedicated to the aspiring writer.

TABLEOFCONTENTS

Introduction	01
Wishful Thinking	04
The Superhero	06
Paper Cranes	09
Abstract Drawing	10
Ode to Dirt	12
The Leaf	14
Skyline at Night	17
1995	20
The Waltz	22
Seeing in Black and White	23

INTRODUCTION

I am on a journey to discover myself as a poet.

I always considered myself more of prose writer or an artist. Poetry was never really my thing. I started writing more poetry in college after taking a writing class. Doing the poetry assignments and reading other poetry helped me learn how to develop my writing.

These poems may not be perfect and I like that about them.

In this series of poems, I wanted to experiment a little. Some of the poems require you to both look and read. The title of this eBook comes from a line in the substructure poem, "Seeing in Black and White". "Wishful Thinking", meant to be a self portrait poem, is another poem where I tried to think outside the box and make something that seemed not like a poem into a poem. Another of my favorites is "The Waltz", a simple short ironic poem. I loved trying to make a memorable poem using just a few lines. All the poems hold meaning to me.

I hope you find a poem or two that means something to you.

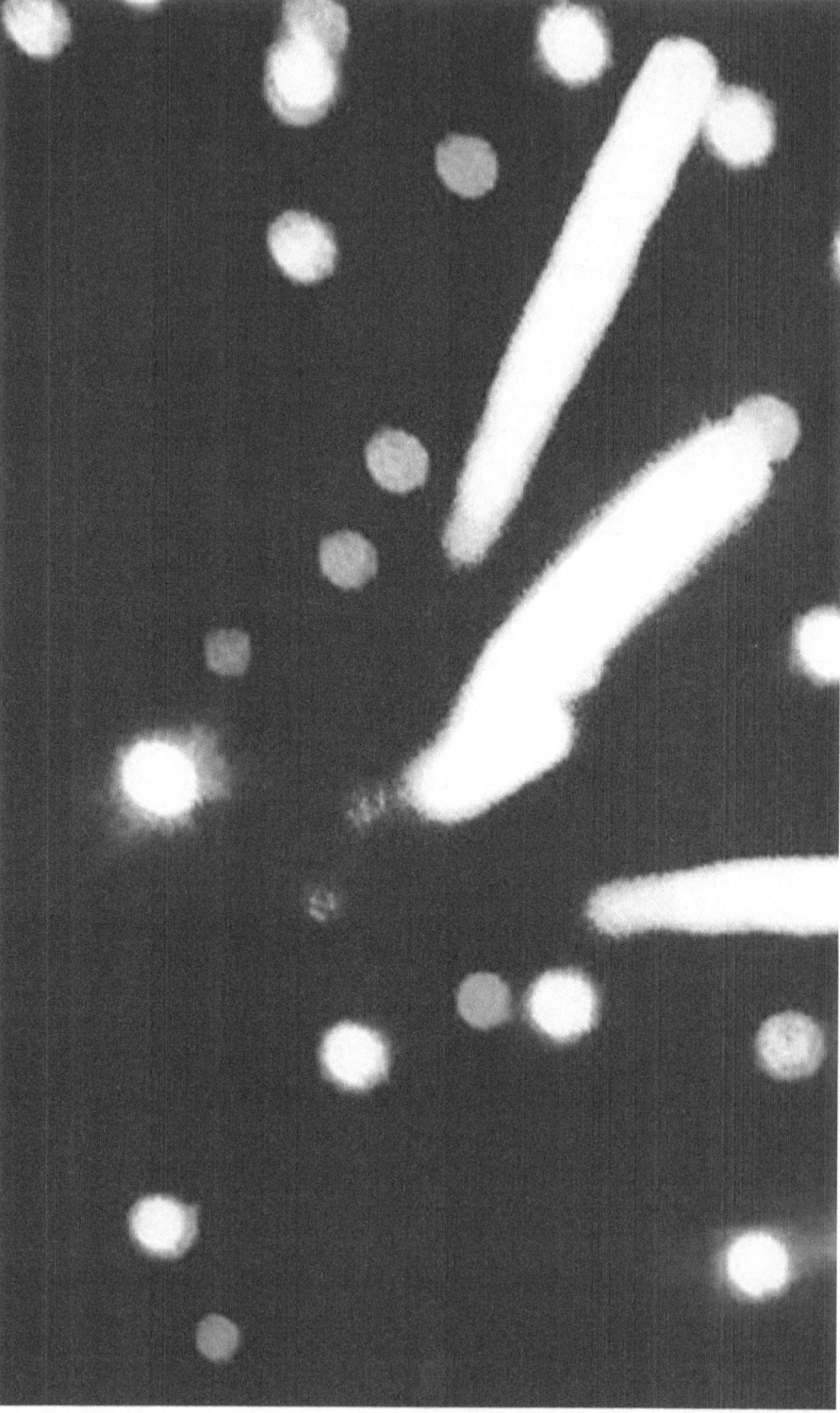

WISHFULTHINKING
(20 Things I Want to Do Before I Die)

Get married.
~~Study abroad in Italy.~~
Learn to speak a foreign language.
~~Go to college.~~

~~Write a book and get it published.~~
Learn to stop procrastinating.
See a lunar eclipse at night.
~~Attend a major sporting event.~~

Be an extra in a movie.
Watch a movie in a drive-in.
Ride inside a hot air balloon.
~~Ride something bigger than a horse.~~

Go to an activist protest.
Shower under a waterfall.
Cross a country on bicycle.
~~Drive a boat on Lake Michigan.~~

04

~~Cast my vote in an election.~~
Meet a famous politician.
Be a hero in somebody's life.
Accept myself for who I am.

THE SUPERHERO

Though the spotlight shines on me
and the public claims me as a hero,
I hide behind this costume
because I am afraid
to reveal who I really am.

My elaborately decorated mask
is made just for my face,
carefully fitted costume
with bright and coordinated colors
that strangers imitate
and worship.

Without the mask,
I am a man without purpose.
Though the powers I have
are real,
they separate me from
the rest of the world.
I am not just a savior,
but an outcast.

I have saved
many lives,
but I am only remembered
for the villains I have
won against
and not the lives
that have been lost
because of my fights,
the victims who were
forgotten.

I am afraid to let them
see who I am
beneath the
acts of heroism.

In my real life
I am just another person
who needs to be saved.

PAPERCRANES

I fold them slowly, meditatively;
the colorful paper is delicate
like the fragility of your body
that's entering into it's dying state.

An ancient legend of the Japanese
says, if I make a thousand paper cranes,
the mystical beast can end your disease
so I fold creases to ease all our pain.

The crane's power to live to a thousand
can't change your mortality,
but I still wonder if I can finish
folding in time to wish for you to heal.

A B S T R A C T D R A W I N G
(2008, mixed media, not quite finished)

Passing through the room it waits alone in,
you can not help but be captured by it.
Layers of shape bounce against the page as
vibrant hues of colors remind me of
a carnival filled with life and mystery.

A soft tangerine glides in the background,
a green and blue line twists around the edge,
turquoise fills in colored lines to form shapes
while short violet lines dance together.

Red boxes in the bottom right corner
have swirled lines flowing out of them,
pink and green lines intertwine in a circle,
a smeared coral blade pointing to it.

Black lines fall across the top left corner
as white paint sweeps across shapes and colors
as if to erase some areas,
but instead blending textures together.

I see a roller coaster in the green and blue line,
a hopscotch game in red chalk in place of boxes,
ponds in the bright blue shapes,
grass blades in the wind instead of violet lines.

A closer look reveals written words
hidden messages beneath layers of shapes,
like graffiti in a tunnel beneath the city.

Suddenly, the artwork transforms in to
a green and blue jellyfish swimming on top,
flowers blooming out of planter boxes,
a shooting white star bleeding across
oceans of colors,

waiting for its chance to come alive,
for strangers to see their worlds in it.

ODE TO DIRT

Abused every day,
it sleeps beneath you,
branded with footprints.

It's soft, bistre body
is often interpreted
as wasted instead of
precious.

Even though our planet is named after it,
it's name is mocked and used
to describe the ugliest things.

In return for your ignorance,
it gives back
food for your family,
roses for your lover,
sunflowers for your kitchen,
vibrant surroundings.

It takes anything put into it,
and gives it life,
allowing it
to blossom.

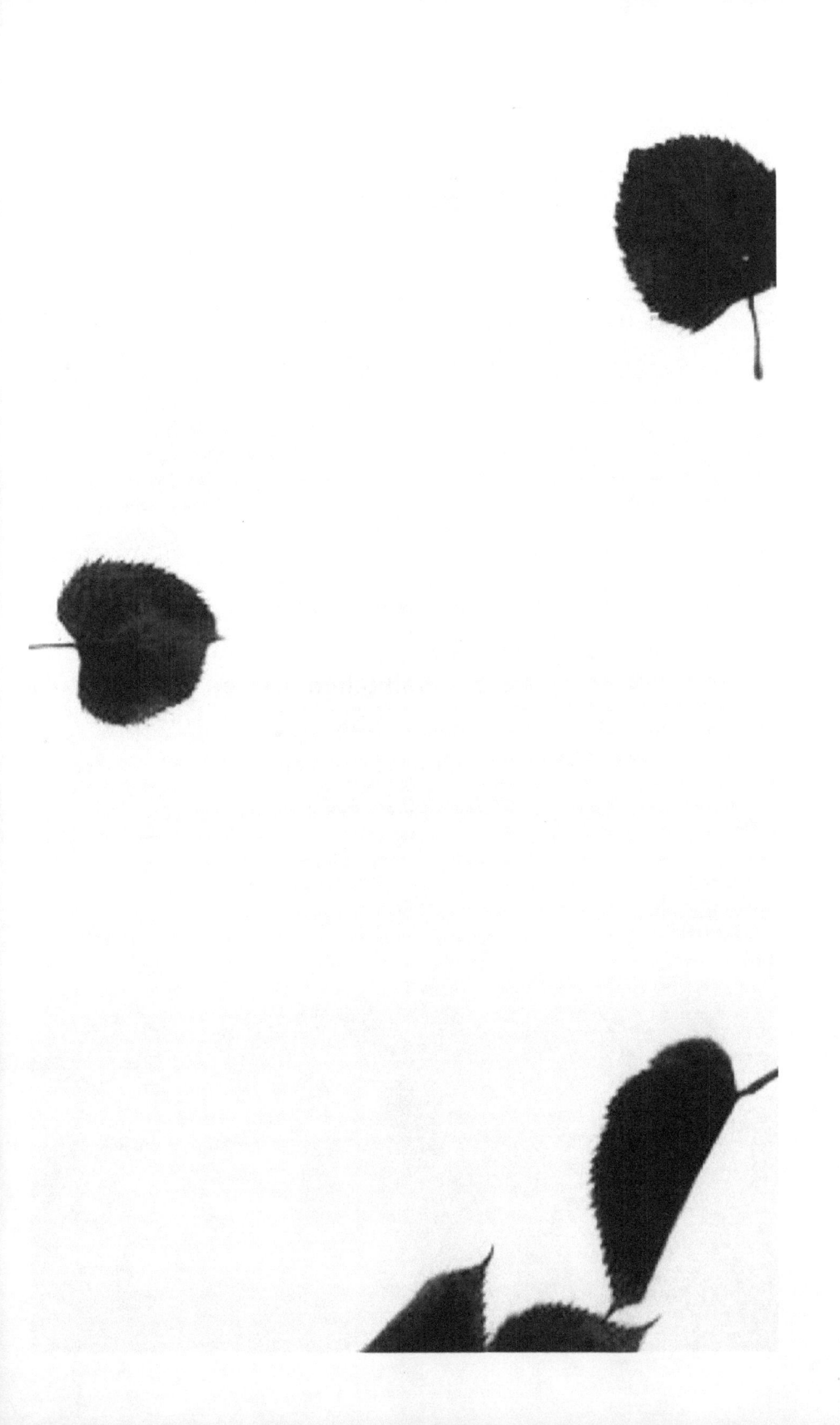

THE LEAF

It glides to the ground,
painted colors of a sunset
with singed edges.
Yellow hues mimic aged paper,
its soft veins sketched
in taupe graphite.

Crumpled and delicate,
like an old letter thrown away
after years hiding in a drawer,
the leaf is unaware
it is decaying for the rebirth
of nature in spring.

SKYLINEATNIGHT
(over Chicago)

Light glows through tiny windows
of what look like
plastic toys from here.
Painted blue and violet sky
is a backdrop in the time
just between morning and night.

I sit in a stiff airplane seat
next to a stranger
thousands of feet above the ground,
yet I feel comfort.
The city is asleep,
but I am wide awake.

With my hand against the small window,
my fingers trace highways
that I usually avoid.
My thumb is the same height
as one of the tallest
skyscrapers in the world.
my hand.

The patterns of buildings and lights,
rows of miniature homes,
and streets connecting communities
show me structure and stability
in a city of chaos and crime.
A city that has brought chaos to me.

A blinking light and loudspeaker
reminding me to fasten my seatbelt
brings me back to the reality of
uncomfortable seating
and distressed passengers,
but I am ready to face the world,
remembering for just a minute
I held the city in

1995

The gold jewelry box waited for me
next to the old fashioned piano that sang
our music back to us from a piano roll,
in the basement we used to play in.

My grandma's photographs hung on walls
near collections of glass animals
and carved statues that guarded rooms
of her one-story house in Dayton.

While my parents and relatives
fought like children over which items
were theirs, my sister and I split
the hand painted glass frogs equally.

The black stallion you could see from
the kitchen now hangs in our living room,
while the piano player in the basement
went to my cousins.

The black stallion you could see from
the kitchen now hangs in our living room,
while the piano player in the basement
went to my cousins.

Nobody argued over the little
box in the basement,
its tiny white beads
and gold interior
holding inside
my memories of her.

THE WALTZ

I hesitate to follow your steps
as you try to lead me
on the path I was warned about.

But when the music plays,
you hold my hands
and we move as one.

(Seeing in Black and White)

IREADTHENEW
SARTICLETHAT
SAIDALLTHOSEP
EOPLEHADDIEDFI
GHTINGFOROURC
OUNTRYANDITHOU
GHTANEYEFORANE
YEONLYLEADSTOBLINDNESS

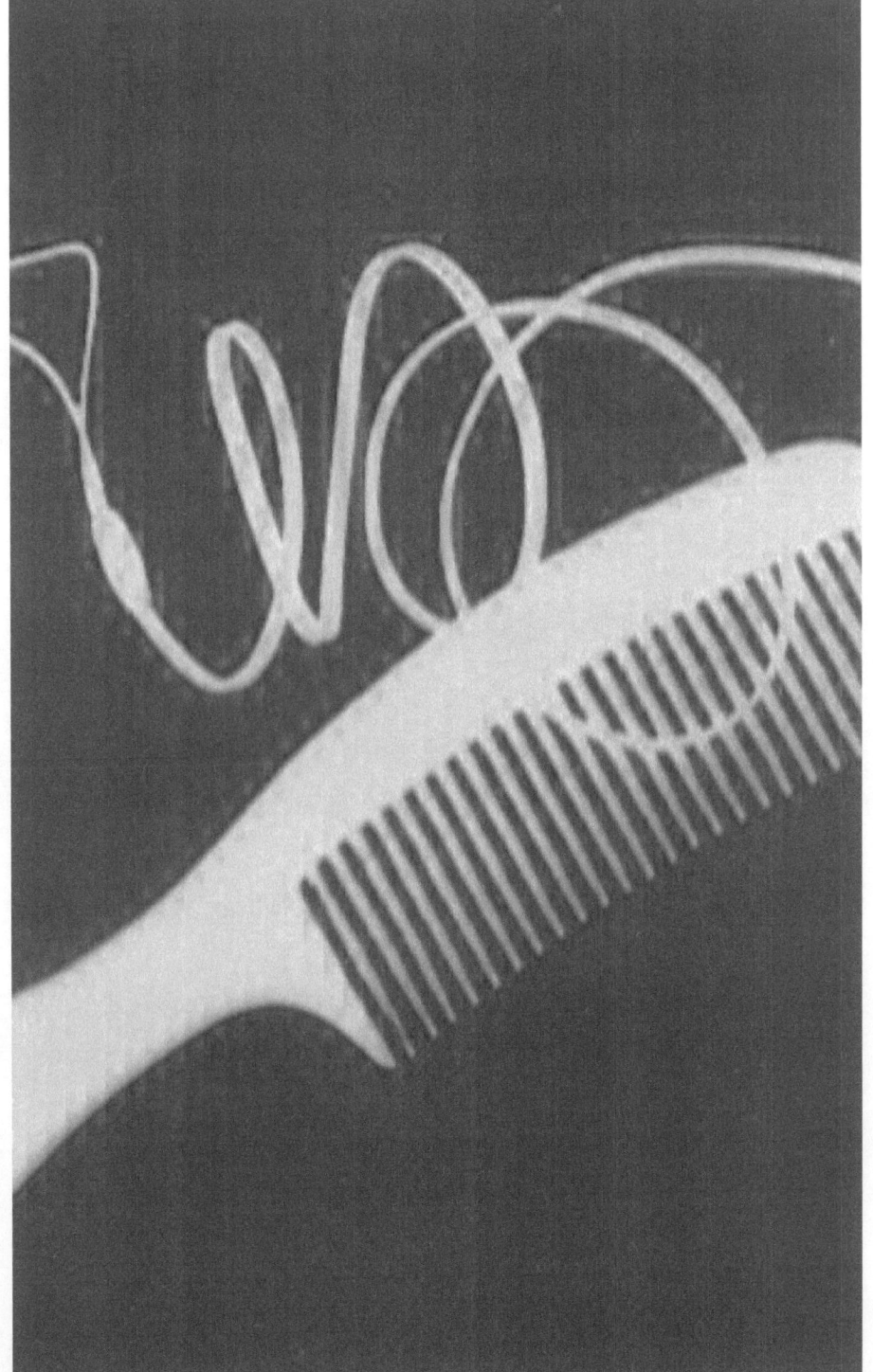

ABOUT THE AUTHOR

Anna Leehey currently lives in Chicago with her cat, Lea. She wrote and took all photos in this book. You can find more boosk as well as her artwork on her website at annaleehey.com

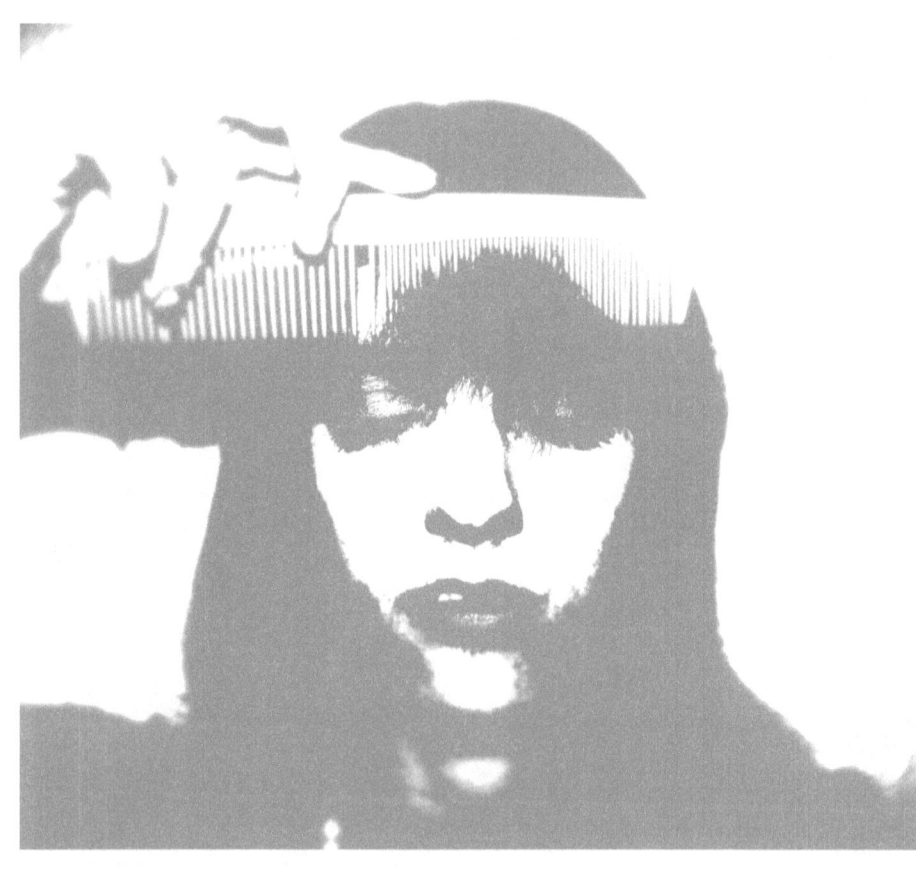

www.ingramcontent.com/pod-product-compliance
Lightning Source LLC
Chambersburg PA
CBHW031516210526
45464CB00007B/2939